NORTH AMERICA

by
Grace Jones

Image Credits

All images are courtesy of Shutterstock.com, unless otherwise specified. With thanks to Getty Images, Thinkstock Photo and iStockphoto.
Front Cover – Andriy Blokhin, miker, Sylvie Bouchard. 1 – kavram. 4&5 – metha1819. 6&7 – blew_s, Rich Carey, Artur Balytskyi. 8&9 – Uwe Bergwitz, Mikhail Kolesnikov. 10&11 – Andriy Blokhin, miker, Evgeniapp, PhotocechCZ, Anan Kaewkhammul, Sorayot Chinkanjanarot, Vladimir Wrangel, Schnapps2012, Tom Tietz. 12&13 – Vesna Kriznar, rodimov, bimserd. 14&15 – Kwadrat, Warren Metcalf, Betty Shelton. 16&17 – chris kolaczan, TalyaPhoto, Howard Sandler. 18&19 – Evgeniapp, Rich Carey, Prentiss. 20&21 – Konstantin Tronin, Sveta Imnadze. 22&23 – Kurt M, Bruce MacQueen, Kerry Hargrove. 24&25 – kojihirano, Kwadrat, Joseph Sohm. 26&27 – Kametaro, pinkomelet, Michael Gordon, arikbintang, a katz, ESB Professional.

BookLife
PUBLISHING

©2018
BookLife Publishing
King's Lynn
Norfolk PE30 4LS

A catalogue record for this book is available from the British Library.

ISBN: 978-1-78637-246-8

Written by:
Grace Jones

Edited by:
John Wood

Designed by:
Drue Rintoul

CONTENTS

Words that look like this are explained in the glossary on page 30.

ENDANGERED ANIMALS

Experts estimate that there are anywhere between two million and nine million **species** living on planet Earth today, but thousands of these are in danger of dying out every single year.

WHAT DOES IT MEAN IF A SPECIES IS ENDANGERED?

Any species of plant or animal that is at risk of dying out completely is said to be endangered. When all individuals of a single species die, that species has become extinct. Extinction is a real possibility for all species that are already threatened or endangered. Experts estimate that between 150 and 200 different species become extinct every day.

Dinosaurs are an example of an extinct species. They walked the Earth over 225 million years ago and became extinct around 65 million years ago.

The International Union for Conservation of Nature and Natural Resources (IUCN) is the main **organisation** that records which species are in danger of extinction. The species are put into different categories, from the most to the least threatened with extinction.

IUCN'S CATEGORIES OF THREATENED ANIMALS

Category	Explanation
Extinct	Species that have no surviving members
Extinct in the Wild	Species with only surviving members in **captivity**
Critically Endangered	Species that have an extremely high risk of extinction in the wild
Endangered	Species that have a high risk of extinction in the wild
Vulnerable	Species that are likely to become endangered or critically endangered in the near future
Near Threatened	Species that are likely to become vulnerable or endangered in the near future
Least Concern	Species that fit into none of the above categories

The Javan rhinoceros has been categorised by the IUCN as 'critically endangered', with around 46-66 individuals remaining in the wild.

The IUCN's work is extremely important. Once a species has been recognised as 'at risk', organisations and **governments** will often take steps to protect the species and its **habitats** in order to save it from extinction. The practice of protecting or saving a species and its habitats is called **conservation**.

WHY DO ANIMALS BECOME ENDANGERED?

Over the last 100 years, the human **population** of the world has grown by over 4.5 billion people. As the population has grown, the damage humans do to the **environment** and wildlife has increased too. Many experts believe that human activity is the biggest threat to animals around the world today.

Habitat Destruction

One of the biggest threats species face is the loss of their habitats. Large areas of land are often used to build **settlements** to provide more housing, food and **natural resources** for the growing world population. This can often destroy natural habitats, which nearby wildlife need in order to survive.

To use land for housing or farming, all the trees must be cut down and cleared from the area. This is called **deforestation**.

THE WORLD WIDE FUND FOR NATURE (WWF) ESTIMATES THAT BETWEEN 200 AND 2,000 SPECIES OF ANIMAL BECOME EXTINCT EVERY SINGLE YEAR.

POLLUTION

Pollution is the introduction of harmful waste to the air, water or land. Pollution threatens wildlife all over the world. For example, people drop litter, which can cut, choke or even poison animals.

HUNTERS AND POACHERS

Many species are endangered because of hunting or **poaching**. Throughout history, humans have hunted certain species of animal, usually for their meat, fur, skin or tusks.

The dodo was a species of bird that was hunted to extinction. The last time a dodo was seen alive was in 1662.

Male African elephants are hunted by poachers for their huge tusks, which are made from a natural material called ivory and are sold for lots of money.

Natural Causes

While the most serious threats to animals are caused by humans, there are natural threats to animals too. For example, it is thought that the extinction of the dinosaurs was caused by a natural event, when a **meteorite** hit the Earth. Other species may become extinct because they are not as well **adapted** to survive in their environments as others. Experts believe that the number of species that become extinct due to human activity is around 1,000 times more than those becoming extinct through natural causes.

NORTH AMERICA

North America is one of the seven continents of the world. Continents are large areas of land that, along with the five oceans, make up the Earth's surface. The other six continents are: Africa, Antarctica, Asia, Australia, Europe and South America.

North America is the third biggest continent in the world. There are three oceans that surround North America. The Atlantic Ocean lies on the east coast of North America, the Pacific Ocean to the west and the Arctic Ocean to the north.

CONTINENTS OF THE WORLD

DO YOU KNOW WHICH CONTINENT YOU LIVE IN?

ARCTIC OCEAN

NORTH AMERICA

ATLANTIC OCEAN

EUROPE

ASIA

PACIFIC OCEAN

AFRICA

PACIFIC OCEAN

SOUTH AMERICA

INDIAN OCEAN

AUSTRALIA

ANTARCTIC OCEAN

ANTARCTICA

FACTS ABOUT NORTH AMERICA

FACTFILE

Population: Over 529 million people.

Land Area: Over 24.7 million square kilometres (km).

Countries: 23

Highest Peak: Denali in the United States of America (USA) rises to 6,190 metres (m) above sea level.

Longest River: The Missouri river is the longest river in North America and it is over 3,700 km long.

Biggest Country by Area: Canada, which is over 9.9 million square km.

Main Languages Spoken: English and Spanish.

Denali

Wildlife and Habitats

There are many different types of habitat found across the North American continent such as tropical rainforests, woodlands, deserts and **marine** habitats. North America is home to many species that are not found anywhere else in the world. The continent has an estimated 457 mammal species, 914 bird species, 662 reptile species and more than 300 species of amphibian.

Yosemite National Park, USA, is one of the many national parks found across North America

ENDANGERED NORTH AMERICAN ANIMALS

Currently, there are over 1,200 species of animal listed as endangered or threatened in North America. The biggest threats that these species face come from human activity. The effects of deforestation, pollution and habitat destruction are threatening wildlife across North America.

10 ANIMALS IN DANGER IN EUROPE

1

California Condor

Conservation Status:
Critically Endangered

Number:
Around 100 adults in the wild

2

Boreal Woodland Caribou

Conservation Status:
Threatened

Number:
Unknown

3

Kemp's Ridley Sea Turtle

Conservation Status:
Critically Endangered

Number:
Unknown

4

Red Wolf

Conservation Status:
Critically Endangered

Number:
Between 50-75

5

Cougar

Conservation Status:
Least Concern

Number:
Unknown

6

Black-Footed Ferret

Conservation Status:
Endangered

Number:
Around 200 adults left
in the wild

7

Wood Bison

Conservation Status:
Near Threatened

Number:
Around 11,000

8

Townsend's Big-Eared Bat

Conservation Status:
Least Concern

Number:
Unknown

9

Steller Sea Lion

Conservation Status:
Near Threatened

Number:
Over 81,000 adults in the wild

10

Bighorn Sheep

Conservation Status:
Least Concern

Number:
Around 60,000

CALIFORNIA CONDOR

FACTFILE

Number Living in the Wild: Around 100 adults

IUCN Status: Critically Endangered

Scientific Name: *Gymnogyps californianus*

Weight: Up to 12 kilograms (kg)

Size: It has a wingspan of around 3 m

Life Span: Around 60 years

Habitat: Rocky **scrublands**, forests and mountains

Diet: **Carnivore**

California Condor

Where Do They Live?

The California condor can be found in rocky scrublands, forests and mountains in southern and central California and Arizona. However, the California condor used to live throughout the whole of the western USA from Canada to Mexico.

Key

- Oceans and Seas
- Land
- California Condor Habitats

Pacific Ocean

NORTH AMERICA

Atlantic Ocean

WHY ARE THEY IN DANGER?

California condor populations decreased during the 20th century because of hunting. While the California condor is not usually a target, its **prey** is. California condors will eat dead animals that have been shot and killed by hunters. The bullets used to shoot the animals are often made of lead, which is poisonous once eaten. Over time California condors can **ingest** so much lead that they die from lead poisoning.

How Are They Being Protected?

Much has been done to **legally** protect California condors from lead poisoning. The Ridley-Tree Condor Preservation Act in 2007 banned the use of lead bullets within California in the hope of stopping lead poisoning altogether. There have also been conservation efforts to **breed** California condors in captivity. Over 154 California condors that have been bred in captivity have been released back into the wild in recent years.

IT IS THOUGHT THAT OVER ONE THIRD OF CALIFORNIA CONDORS ARE EXPERIENCING THE EFFECTS OF LEAD POISONING.

A California Condor Chick

COUGAR

Number Living in the Wild: Unknown

IUCN Status: Least Concern

Scientific Name: *Puma concolor*

Weight: Males usually weigh around 62 kg and females 42 kg

Size: Males are usually around 2.4 m long and females 2 m long

Life Span: Between 8-13 years in the wild

Habitat: Forests, rainforests and mountain deserts

Diet: Carnivore

Cougars, also known as pumas or mountain lions, live in both the North American and the South American continents.

Where Do They Live?

Cougars live in forests, rainforests and mountain deserts. Cougars used to live all over the North American continent, but now they only live on the west coast of the USA, in Canada and in parts of Central America.

Key

- Oceans and Seas
- Land
- Cougar Habitats

Pacific Ocean

NORTH AMERICA

Atlantic Ocean

Why Are They in Danger?

Hunting is the biggest threat that cougars face today. Cougars often eat farmer's **livestock** and they are dangerous to humans as they have killed a number of people in Canada and the USA in recent years. For these reasons, they are often hunted and killed by humans. Because it is still legal to hunt cougars in many western states in the USA and Canada, cougar numbers are continuing to decrease.

Cougar

COUGARS THAT LIVE IN FLORIDA ARE OFTEN KILLED ON THE BUSY ROADS BY CARS OR LORRIES.

HOW ARE THEY BEING PROTECTED?

Cougars are legally protected in California and much of Central America, including Guatemala, Honduras, Nicaragua, Costa Rica and Panama. Cougars are also partly protected in Canada and the USA by hunting **regulations**. However, much more needs to be done to increase the level of protection cougars have in many states across the USA and Canada to save the population from future extinction.

BOREAL WOODLAND CARIBOU

FACTFILE

Number Living in the Wild: Unknown

IUCN Status: Threatened

Scientific Name: *Rangifer tarandus caribou*

Weight: Between 110–320 kg

Size: Around 1.8 m long

Life Span: Between 10-15 years in the wild

Habitat: Woodland forests filled with **lichen**

Diet: **Herbivore**

Boreal Woodland Caribou

Where Do They Live?

Boreal woodland caribou live in woodland forests across northern Canada. They prefer to live in small groups and stay in the forest for most of the year.

Key

- Oceans and Seas
- Land
- Boreal Woodland Caribou Habitats

Pacific Ocean

NORTH AMERICA

Atlantic Ocean

Orange Lichens

WHY ARE THEY IN DANGER?

Boreal woodland caribou populations have been affected by habitat loss over recent years. They need large areas of forest that can support the growth of the lichen that they feed on. Deforestation is occurring in many of their habitats so the land can be used for mining, **logging**, and the construction of roads. All of these factors have contributed to habitat loss and the decline of the boreal woodland caribou population.

How Are They Being Protected?

Environment Canada is currently developing a plan for increasing boreal woodland caribou populations in Canada. While this is still in development, education and awareness have become important tools to help caribou recovery and encourage conservation action. Parks Canada is leading the way in conservation education and provides lessons on the importance of protecting boreal woodland caribou and their habitats.

IF BOREAL WOODLAND CARIBOU ARE NOT BETTER PROTECTED THEY MAY BECOME EXTINCT BY THE YEAR 2100.

KEMP'S RIDLEY SEA TURTLE

FACTFILE

Number Living in the Wild: Unknown

IUCN Status: Critically Endangered

Scientific Name: *Lepidochelys kempii*

Weight: Around 45 kg

Size: Around 65 centimetres (cm) long

Life Span: Around 50 years in the wild

Habitat: Marine

Diet: Omnivore

Kemp's Ridley Sea Turtle

Where Do They Live?

Kemp's ridley sea turtles live in shallow waters in marine habitats mostly in the Gulf of Mexico and the northern Atlantic Ocean.

Key

- Oceans and Seas
- Land
- Kemp's Ridley Sea Turtle Habitats

Pacific Ocean

NORTH AMERICA

Atlantic Ocean

Gulf of Mexico

TODAY, IT IS ESTIMATED THAT THERE ARE ONLY 1,000 BREEDING FEMALES LEFT IN THE WILD.

Why Are They in Danger?

The Kemp's ridley sea turtle has been on the Endangered Species List since 1970. The population has declined over the last century because their eggs have been **harvested** and many adults have been killed for their meat and skin. Recently, **commercial fishing** has also damaged the population. Kemp's ridley sea turtles can easily become caught in the types of nets used by commercial fisheries. When they become caught, they are unable to come to the surface of the water to breathe.

This is a gillnet, which is a type of fishing net that is responsible for the deaths of many Kemp's ridley sea turtles over the years.

THE KEMP'S RIDLEY SEA TURTLE IS THE MOST ENDANGERED SPECIES OF TURTLE IN THE WORLD.

HOW ARE THEY BEING PROTECTED?

The Mexican government had taken a number of steps to conserve the Kemp's ridley sea turtle. In 1990, a law was passed to protect all sea turtles. The only known nesting site of the Kemp's ridley sea turtle, at Rancho Nuevo beach, has also been protected. In the USA, the US Fish and Wildlife Service and the National Marine Fisheries Service have worked together to reduce the number of turtles being caught in nets by changing the most damaging fishing practices. Conservation efforts between the USA and Mexico have led to increased numbers of Kemp's ridley sea turtles.

RED WOLF

FACTFILE

Number Living in the Wild: Between 50–75

IUCN Status: Critically Endangered

Scientific Name: *Canis rufus*

Weight: Between 20–36 kg

Size: Around 65 cm tall

Life Span: Between 6–7 years in the wild

Habitat: Woodlands, swamps and **prairies**

Diet: Carnivore

Red Wolves

Where Do They Live?

Red wolves used to live throughout south-eastern USA, but now they only live in a small area in north-eastern North Carolina.

Key

- Oceans and Seas
- Land
- Red Wolf Habitats

Pacific Ocean

NORTH AMERICA

Atlantic Ocean

WHY ARE THEY IN DANGER?

The main threat to the survival of the red wolf is hybridisation. Hybridisation is when an animal of one species breeds with an animal of another species. For many years, red wolves have bred with coyotes. The young that the two species produce together are hybrids and are no longer categorised as red wolves. If hybridisation continues to occur, red wolves will soon become extinct.

Red Wolf-Coyote Hybrid

How Are They Being Protected?

A conservation programme began in the 1970s to breed red wolves in captivity and there are now nearly 200 of them! To stop hybridisation from occurring, 102 red wolves that have been bred in captivity were reintroduced to north-eastern North Carolina in 1987. At that time, the area was free of coyotes, but during the 1990s coyotes spread to North Carolina. **Conservationists** must find new locations for the red wolf to live in and new ways to tackle hybridisation if the red wolf is to survive in the future.

Red wolves are also threatened by busy roads where they can be hit and killed by moving vehicles.

21

BLACK-FOOTED FERRET

FACTFILE

Number Living in the Wild: Around 200 adults left in the wild

IUCN Status: Endangered

Scientific Name: *Mustela nigripes*

Weight: Between 600 grams–1.1 kg

Size: Between 45–64 cm long

Life Span: Between 3–4 years in the wild

Habitat: Grasslands and scrublands where prairie dogs live

Diet: Carnivore

Black-Footed Ferret

Where Do They Live?

Black-footed ferrets once lived across North America from southern Canada to northern Mexico, but became extinct in the wild in 1986. They have now been reintroduced into the wild and live in northern USA.

Key

■ Oceans and Seas
■ Land
■ Black-Footed Ferret Habitats

NORTH AMERICA

Pacific Ocean

Atlantic Ocean

Why Are They in Danger?

During the 20th century, black-footed ferrets depended upon prairie dogs for food. However, many prairie dogs were killed by farmers because they were damaging their crops. This left the black-footed ferrets with less prey to eat and many died because they did not have enough food. More recently, prairie dog and black-footed ferret populations have decreased because of a disease called sylvatic plague. Once they become infected with this disease, they often die. These two reasons meant that, by 1986, the black-footed ferret had become almost extinct in the wild.

A Black-Tailed Prairie Dog

HOW ARE THEY BEING PROTECTED?

In 1985, a conservation programme began to breed black-footed ferrets in captivity. So far, over 8,000 members have been bred in captivity. Some of these members have been reintroduced back into the wild in eight states in the USA, one site in Canada and one site in Mexico. Conservation efforts have also included research into a cure for sylvatic plague, although this could take a long time to find. Even if the cure is found, it would take a very long time to **vaccinate** all members of a species.

NORTH AMERICA IN THE FUTURE

Many steps have already been taken to protect wildlife and conserve habitats throughout North America, but much more can still be done to save endangered animals from future extinction.

Laws and Governments

Governments across North America have come together in recent years to work together to conserve their most endangered animals.

However, much more needs to be done to protect endangered species such as the cougar. Cougars can still be legally hunted in most states in the USA and Canada. While hunters have to follow hunting regulations, cougars need full legal protection if they are to be saved from future extinction.

Wildlife tourists like these ones here at San Diego Zoo help to protect wildlife and conserve habitats.

WILDLIFE TOURISM

Many wildlife organisations, charities and governments around the world are using the money that is made from **wildlife tourism** to protect endangered animals throughout North America. The San Diego Zoo in California, USA, gets over 3.2 million visitors a year. Much of the money that they make from wildlife tourism is used to fund conservation projects throughout North America and the rest of the world. For example, San Diego Zoo began a breeding programme in 1982 to increase the numbers of the California condor. Since then they have successfully bred 165 California condors in captivity.

HOW CAN I MAKE A DIFFERENCE?

1 CAMPAIGN WITH AN ORGANISATION

Wildlife organisations such as WWF and Greenpeace have helped to save many endangered species and even convince countries to change the laws through campaigning.

2 DONATE TO A CHARITY YOU BELIEVE IN

You can usually donate as little or as much as you want. Most charities show you how your donations are helping to make a difference.

3 LEARN MORE ABOUT ENDANGERED SPECIES IN YOUR AREA

One of the most important ways to protect endangered species is by understanding the threats that they face. Visit a local wildlife refuge, national park or reserve or join a local wildlife organisation.

4 ADOPT AN ANIMAL

Your donation will normally go to feeding and looking after the animal that you have adopted. You'll usually get an adoption certificate and regular updates on how your animal is doing.

5 HELP TO RAISE AWARENESS BY TALKING TO OTHERS

It is important that we all talk about issues that may threaten wildlife throughout the world. By talking about these issues, it can help to make people aware of how they may be affecting wildlife and encourage them to take steps to prevent harm.

6 VOLUNTEER AT A LOCAL WILDLIFE CHARITY OR SHELTER

It is not only endangered animals who need our help; we should help to take care of all the animals in the world.

FIND OUT MORE

To find out more about endangered species in North America and what you can do to get involved with conservation efforts, visit:

International Union for Conservation of Nature (IUCN)
www.iucnredlist.org

San Diego Zoo
zoo.sandiegozoo.org

World Wide Fund for Nature (WWF)
www.worldwildlife.org

To discover more about other endangered animals around the world take a look at more books in this series:

Antarctica, Endangered Animals
Grace Jones (BookLife, 2018)

Asia, Endangered Animals
Grace Jones (BookLife, 2018)

Australia, Endangered Animals
Grace Jones (BookLife, 2018)

Africa, Endangered Animals
Grace Jones (BookLife, 2018)

Europe, Endangered Animals
Grace Jones (BookLife, 2018)

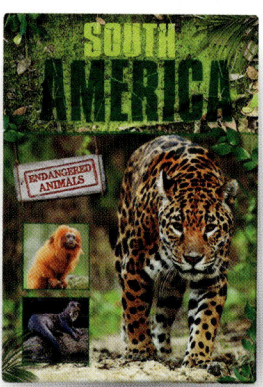

South America, Endangered Animals
Grace Jones (BookLife, 2018)

QUICK QUIZ

1. HOW MANY CALIFORNIA CONDORS ARE LIVING IN THE WILD?

2. WHAT IS THE SCIENTIFIC NAME OF THE COUGAR?

3. WHAT DO BLACK-FOOTED FERRETS FEED ON?

4. HOW MUCH DO BOREAL WOODLAND CARIBOU WEIGH?

5. HOW LONG DO KEMP'S RIDLEY SEA TURTLES USUALLY LIVE FOR?

6. WHAT IS THE IUCN CONSERVATION STATUS OF THE RED WOLF?

For answers see the bottom of page 32.

GLOSSARY

adapted	changed over time to suit different conditions
breed	the process of producing young
captivity	animals that are cared for by humans and not living in the wild
carnivore	animals that eat other animals rather than plants
commercial fishing	fishing companies who make money from large-scale fishing
conservation	the practice of protecting or conserving a species and its habitats
conservationists	people who act for the protection of wildlife and the environment
deforestation	the action of cutting down trees on large areas of land
environment	the natural world
governments	groups of people with the authority to run countries and decide their laws
habitats	the natural environments in which animals or plants live
harvested	gathered by humans to eat
herbivore	an animal that only eats plants
ingest	to take into the body by swallowing
legally	performed within the limits of the law

lichen	an algae and a fungus living together to create a new living thing
livestock	animals that are kept for farming purposes
logging	the activity of cutting down trees to be used for timber
marine	relating to the sea
meteorite	a piece of rock that successfully enters a planet's atmosphere without being destroyed
natural resources	useful materials that are created by nature
omnivore	an animal that eats plants and other animals
organisation	a group of people that work together to achieve the same goals
poaching	the act of the illegal capturing or killing of wild animals
population	the number of people living in a place
prairies	large open areas of grassland
prey	animals that are hunted by other animals for food
regulations	rules
scrublands	lands with shrubs or small trees on them
settlements	places people live permanently, like villages or towns
species	a group of very similar animals or plants that are capable of producing young together
vaccinate	to treat a disease with a vaccine
wildlife tourism	the actions and industry behind attracting people to visit new places to see wildlife

INDEX

1. Around 100 adults in the wild **2.** Puma concolor **3.** Prairie dogs
4. Between 110–320 kg **5.** 50 years in the wild **6.** Critically Endangered